ADRIFT
ON
BLINDING
LIGHT

Also by PAUL PINES

POETRY

Onion
Hotel Madden Poems
Pines Songs
Breath

NOVELS

The Tin Angel
Redemption

ADRIFT
ON
BLINDING LIGHT

Paul Pines

Photographs by
Josephine Sacebo

To Barbara
with gratitude -
6·8·08

IKON
New York, New York

Work from this collection has appeared in following journals:
*New Directions, Ironwood, Pequod, Confrontation, City, First
Intensity, House Organ, Adirondack Life, Contact II, Sagetrieb,
Cafe Review, Oasia: Broad Side Series, No. 42, SVITO-VYD
(Ukranian trans.), Israel Horizons,* and *IKON.*

"Ossabaw Island Dream," set for mezzo-soprano and chamber
orchestra by composer Daniel Asia, premiered at the Great
Hall in Cooper Union. Asia's settings for "Pines Songs," and
"Songs From The Page of Swords," commissioned and
recorded by bass-baritone John Shirley Quirk, were released on
the *Summit* label.

ISBN: 0-945368-06-2
First Edition

Library of Congress Card Catalogue Number: 2002108826

Cover design by Marisol Limon Martinez and Susan Sherman
from *Hombre Noctámbulo* by Josephine Sacebo

*I would like to express my gratitude to Susan Sherman,
David Unger, Ed and Lorraine Gorn for making this book
possible.*

IKON
151 First Avenue, #46
New York, NY 10003

CONTENTS

OSSABAW ISLAND DREAM

GLYPHS

THE CRY OF MERLIN

DRAGON SMOKE

Photographs by Josephine Sacebo

Cover design from Hombre Noctámbulo

OSSABAW ISLAND DREAM

> *How can we*
> *offer it all, Paul? how*
> *ignore the earth movers . will*
> *take it all down?*

Paul Blackburn, *THE JOURNALS*

1

To say I've come back from the dead
Is to say...what?
that this morning I woke
to birds singing in palmettos
or that I dreamed my friends
were unhappy, most of the women
jumping out of windows
and I was back
on Avenue B
living on chicken hearts
and old soup in a dirty room
thinking,
            "Clean this place up and write
something about loneliness:
where it leads and how it
opens out."

Instead
I fell asleep
and dreamed I woke
to birds singing in palmettos.

To say I've come back from the dead
is to say it feels as if I've risen
from someone else's dream. Who
was I then? He didn't write
a word. Are we really
the same person? All right,
we both woke up
but what happened
to him?

2

I walk around
trying to figure out
how we build up and wear away
until there's nothing left of us.

I cough myself up
from my chest, baiting my breath,
checking my lungs for
congestion. I imagine I appear
as strange to you
as you do to me, coming and going,
trying to find a way
to free ourselves from others' opinions
and still keep in touch. Hard
to be alone. Hard
not to. Coming
and going, sometimes
I think it takes years
to get it right.
Sometimes I think
it's like coming into town
on a Mexican bus
after heavy rain.

Once I came
into Merida that way,
muddy streets washing up
around us, listing
a little like *San Martín*,
a little like a beggar.

3

As a child my dreams
were so vivid
I tried bringing something back
to prove them.

Once I fell asleep
and met a woman who seemed
to know me better than I knew myself.
She told me that
       the senses overlap
       but not enough to form a single lens
       that will penetrate the heart
       of the matter,
but
to understand
the force which shaped
my life, she said
I must learn to
trust her,
       and I thought,
"Anything this real
 must be true."
Just to be sure
I bent down and picked up a stone
beneath the purple and gold
hem of her skirt.
               I held it so tight
               that after I woke
my palm felt bruised for days.

4

You complain about how hard you work,
life isn't fair, there's never enough
time to do what must be done
and nobody understands
what you do anyway!

You're right.
I agree.

From
the bottom of your eyes
you overwhelm me like a single color
rising through my world.

I walk away
down the street
have a glass of wine
and wait...
            soon my ears
begin to distinguish
between several
birdsongs

and suddenly
you seem far away
and I realize your despair.

Believe me, my friend,
it is sea-green
and endless.

5

Materials have what we call a memory.
Certain ones
like stone or bronze
have memories that can hold
an impression for
centuries, as in a Kouros
or Mayan glyph-work.
These things appear to know us,
to insist
their memory is an extension
of our own.
We look at the bronze
face of Agamemnon amazed
at his lips
pursed in royal chagrin
down the millenniums,
observe the Reclining Buddha
of Nepal napping
so serenely in the air
we realize the very memory
we breathe
remains hidden
from our experience.
The Laughing Masks of Vera Cruz
roar
with a silent hilarity
that's almost a form
of praise:
what do they care?
We try washing
the memory from our clothes
which finally
appear to remember us anyway.

6

Think of yourself as an idea
through which time is crystallized.

Say you have occurred to yourself
as an idea and time as the silent

architect of its outlines,
say further that you fear

its shape still conforms
to numerous things no longer here.

Consider yourself contained
by a form that seems determined

by absences, to depend upon them.
You ask yourself, *"What am I*

doing in this abstraction as if
it were my experience

and I were just an activity
of time trying to make itself clear?"

7

Do we feel our lives
are more authentic
if we decide someone else
is living through us? I mean
if we say our lives are not
our lives alone but
vehicles for others what
riddle do we pose?

Are we also this other,
the one we recognize? Did
that one recognize itself
as someone else from
another time?

Tell me
is it so dangerous
to be only ourselves
as the crow flies
as the clock ticks we must
practice a deception? Do trees
tell themselves they once
were other trees? Before
this birch was an oak
had it been a cedar
in Lebanon? Does it also
work that way
for stones?

8

There are details I've loved so much
they became a part of me:
        hot Spanish bread,
        the streets of Merida
smelling of earth and stone,

islands nesting
on the Georgia coast
her alluvial skirt hemmed with palms
growing in the arms of oaks,
birds plunging into dark-throated estuaries
and out again
like words breaking
from my throat
as if I were always
fishing.

I had a friend who held
the details of his life so close
as he lay dying he was shocked
to realize he couldn't even take the memory
of his own brown hand
grown leathery in the sun
holding a cigarette.
"It's what love does," he said.
"Nothing you know makes it any different.
You scream going out
the way you scream coming in.
Shit! You don't
ever want to
let go!"

9

Bone Beach

Light changes
faster than you can blink
from bright
to soft coming through a cloud bank
along the shore
where skeleton trees
at low tide
upturned
by shifting dunes
the slow wearing down
the undercutting water
lie
on their sides
limbs and roots broken
and sad
they turn pearl
then gray
except for one
standing upright branches raised
roots dug into wet sand
that reminds me of
an Arkansas family
buried facing each other
as if sitting down
in the earth to share
a long silent meal—
a gesture in which
the dead
tell us
there are some who won't
be washed away

10

How the rain comes,
insistent and slow,
light, distant
over the paddock,
a band of white neon....
                    listen
to it fall,
resurrection fern crawling
on the oak, light and rain together:
it's been this way all week
like a man in a public bathroom
who suddenly gets shy and can't
empty his bladder,
            a few drops
            in the sun, such weather
            as occurs when
            (they say)
            the Devil beats his wife

Arranged on my dresser
comb, brush, Old Spice
and vitamins
            E, B, C,
            and magnesium
            for the kidneys.

My mother's face
turns up in the sink, then drains.
She's going to join my father
as if they never were.

Blackburn said it: "We don't own anything!"
Not our memories.
Not even memories
the dead leave us.
Not a ripple.

Oh, my friends
Let me confess it.
I'm in love
with the prints my feet and fingers make
on everything they touch
and jealous of what waits
behind everything I see:
what I don't see.

What swallows us up.

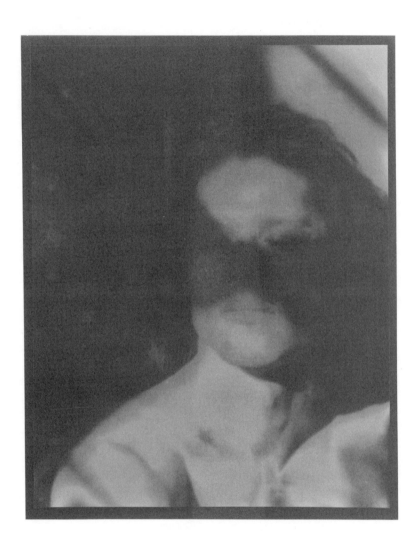

GLYPHS

Writing was a sacred proposition that had the capacity to capture the order of the cosmos, to inform history, to give form to ritual, and to transform the profane material of everyday life into the supernatural.

Linda Schele and David Friedel
A Forest of Kings, The Untold Story of the Ancient Maya

Consider the swimmer
        tangled in eel-grass
            gathering strength
    to break the surface
        for a breath,
    ONE SURGE FOR AIR,
            he figures
        AND THE NEXT TO CALL
        FOR HELP.
There are divers
    in the distance.
Will they see him
        waving from
            his net?
            He sits,
        almost high,
        having spent
his final breath,
        knees pressed in
            the sand,
a Yogi who accepts,
        who views himself
and sees through
        his distress
            the current move,
the light develop
        a clear and timeless
            syntax.

They're moving the fixtures out of THAU'S.

They're carrying out the stool
on which Edith-of-the-Swollen-Feet
sat nursing her edema.

Where the stove had been
against the wall
a heavy plaque of grease.

Max says,

> *"Hey, Paul, you want the mirrors
> or a piece of the counter?"*

This is how it ends,
52 years of food encrustation
and intelligent life adrift in the soup.

ECCE HOMO

Great men
who go mad
are always
raving about
their private habits.
Nietzsche
writes
an essay
called, "Why I Am So Great"
in which
he tells us
what he had for breakfast!

Well,
today I sautéed onions
in lemon-butter
and simmered
with snails
       on my own stove
       above 2nd Avenue
       the sun at its zenith
       drunk as a lord.

Clouds over Bellevue lined with silver.
Rooftops burning like electric cuticles.
Nijinsky believed there was no life on Mars,
said as much clearly
in his diaries
which he signed,

                    "God and Nijinsky."

I want rum
good sweet anise and peppermint.
I want to drive bumper-cars in Coney Island.
I want to watch pelicans with their heavy wings
             walking up and down the wind.
    I want to write a poem of last words.

There's my cravat
tied to a shaky fixture.
I bought it as a young man in Le Havre
when I fancied myself a Jewish Jack London.
Is this the best I can do for departing splendor,
maroon with white polka-dots?

        Besides,
that fixture
will never hold me. I'll probably
electrocute myself falling off
this cardboard chair.

        To be found fried
on the floor with nothing on but my socks
and a French cravat...shit!
wouldn't that start the rumor-mill turning:

*"He died jerking-off with his light fixture,
but we can't figure out why he was wearing a tie."*

You see
my old Wandering Jew
sends out runners like the plague
and from them more
like himself.

    Or Violet
with her African heart
scarred where drops
have touched her hands that never
reach out.

    And my dreams
that burn by night
and smoke by day in a brain
which, itself, has blossomed
from a node.

Like old men at the baths
beating each other with bay leaves,
their bodies round and pink as children's...
it was the same in Russia
        in the Ukraine
        years ago in Brooklyn,
the same bald heads and varicosities,
road-maps calf high
ending at the knee;
they lie naked on marble slabs,
the conversation is pointless
and easy.

"Who gives a shit about Arthur Schnitzler?"
"Me! I do!"
"So, who are you?"
"Petroleum V. Nasby."
"Ach! Sometimes you're so stupid
it's a pleasure to talk with you."

Tiles sweat,
water in the pool near freezing,
Vulcan in the hot-room in an old felt hat
empties a bucket of water in the furnace,
the coals sigh.
Krishna ripened by the heat,
creased like an old pear in the sun
tells Adonoi:
        "You are everyone in the dream."

Dear Bronk,

Hear! The Voice comes!
And hear the machinery
grind as it slips beyond us,
continues to exist
but disappears
into another sky—
warms itself, perhaps,
but leaves us
dumb
while never
ceasing to affect our lives.

What I've tried to learn
is simply when to listen.
For me that isn't as simple
as it sounds:
          often
a late regret exploding
hurts my ears,
          or the air
seals itself around me
like a drum.
I'm wed and then I am severed.
I comb my hair and rub my eyes.
One day my clothes are pressed,
the next they hang like old flags.

UTOPIA isn't a magnificent place
but a tooting of horns:
         "Look how good I am!"
TOM MOORE,
        playing at celestial wordiness
while the Universe expands and threatens
to explode like an old balloon,
NEWTON,
        space isn't clear
        but a market place
        where the magnetic mobs
        of light and force hawk their wares
        and flout
        your tight-lipped theories of the stars,
EINSTEIN
        you reversible FREUD
        by what light
did you finally see that the structures forming
inside of us
demand completion?

How long did you stare at your image
in the mirror of the firmament
before you understood
        there is never enough time?
        Never!
        Not even for LEONARDO!
        Not even in bad movies!

POLLACK! painting your encephalograph!

Shulamith, my dear...
        Isis in despair
gathered up the severed parts
of her husband,
        Osiris,
fashioned a golden phallus
to replace that fleshy organ
swallowed by a fish.
"My sister, my love," he told her. *"Dry your tears.*
The body is a tomb but your soul will shine
forever in the Dog Star, by which men at sea
will henceforth take their sightings."

Then she left him
by the Nile
stringing nets
and called upon Amon-Ra
who founded her a dynasty:
        Horus,
        a loon who
        ate grapes
        from her breasts,
and Ibis-headed Toth,
kingfisher of bloodstreams.

Stars in my window
lodged where my eyes trapped them
light years ago:
                    cocaine sky,
who said
there'll never be a time-traveler
because there's never been one?
We move in frames like the movies
in images that never disperse.

What if the race survived
to press beyond the speed of light?
Could we return to alter our lives
until they were
as we would have them,
                    leave
our insufficiencies
like so much footage
on the cutting room floor,
                    splice
the terror
from our dreams?

Last night I ran
from my father's house shouting,
"I'll not be buried where I was born!"

I lie down feeling dry though sperm
are moaning in my groin,
get high
and hang-out at the bank
           like Socrates
who said
he'd pay anyone willing
to listen to his foolishness.
(Our common epitaph
might be:
        GIVE IT TO ME IN SINGLES.)

I sing odd songs getting out of bed.
My memory is
        ajar,
        a poke-hole,
        a fat ruse,
        a hollow faith,
        a chancre
        and a snare...
        it signs to me like the Ouija,

HOW MANY LIVES AGO WAS THIS?

Let us consider
the image
& the mirror
all we have
and consciousness
the reflection.

Let us say we
mirror what
we see and grow
as we reflect
more faithfully—

call it
    THE DRAGON and
    THE CIRCLE SQUARED
    an inherent unity
    of mind
    that is the summa
    of our physics.

Let us call it
        WHAT-WE-FEAR
TOWARD-WHICH-WE'RE-DRIVEN.

Pigeons squat
like vultures in trees
that shake their last adornments off
on St. Mark's Church.
            The hour is bare
and in this place
the season is as plain to me
as Ukrainian girls
in parish coats
leafleting for Christ—

    so much time
    over coffee and cigarettes
    waiting for the light
                    of my life
    to leap
    into the world...

            looking out
I note
smoke that trails
from my nose and mouth
isn't smoke,
but the tail of a comet
                that ignites
                in the atmosphere

Frank,

Did I ever tell you
about my discovery?
        The Milky Way
is a restaurant full of Mexicans!

                *

        * SUPER LECHE *
                *

White pillars.
White floors.
And on a white wall in front of me
the clock has a picture of Sir Walter Raleigh
on it...
        the hour
        is half past his face.

I am at the counter
perusing a menu I can't read.
By the time I put it down a blind man
next to me
        has cut his pancakes into
        perfect squares.

If you have learned to distrust continuity
in love, in dreams,

even your oracles will not stand for
your arguments—

which are more continuous than disasters
real or imagined.

Distrust is too easy a word.

Fear is harder; a street the messenger
walks, his old brain

fixed on an objective: stamped
on his sweat shirt

the legend, *DAEDALUS DELIVERS*!

And he does.

I'll never understand
the Universe as music

planets and glands
like notes
on a diatonic scale

the sound of wind
through leaves

tumors in my bloodline

what Pythagoras
listened for until
he found the perfect ratio...

all those years
without so much as a whisper

I was invited to a reunion of the Class of '49.
Inasmuch as I had no social life,
I attended
        and was pleased to be given
dormitory space in the painted desert.

Why did I bring my corduroys?
It seldom went below 90.
                Well, at least
it was integrated,
not to mention infiltrated by my creditors.

It seemed autobiographically sound
I should end up waiting tables.   More so,
that a matron with an autonomous nose
ask me to cover, "The Poor Peoples' Section".
She said it would mean a few dollars difference
to me, but the world to her.

                I agreed,
and introduced myself
as Geronimo
                to the Maitre d',
                a Professor in water-wings
                who lectured me
                on the Deluge.

Andreyev was right:

SCIENCE IS JUST MYSTICISM WITH FACTS.

Which is why we admire
Holmes—
       a seer
       for whom the crime
       is cipher
              (to distill
              and re-enact).
Consider
       Simenon
       and Wollrich,
men who seldom left their rooms,
at the center of their
mysteries
       like clues
  to scenes
blocked before the development of
will or discretion:
  a shock to which the sleeper wakes
  like a murderer in his cell.

If I have grown hawk-like
and hunt alone

zero in
from the heights

strike and re-ascend
with undiminished hunger

that's how it feels to be
touchy and always in need.

A child makes himself a promise
to preserve himself

the man forgets
but the word once given

persists
in the fear of death—

                    that one is dying
                    or already dead

Yesterday I woke with an image
of murder in the courtyard.

Today I look over the parapet
to see blood on the pavement.

Last night my room filled up
with Buddhists who surrounded

me when I tried to flee,
and while their hands reached out

they sang rather lovely birdsongs.

Breakfast at Nick's,
we are all here unbending:

an ambulance medic named Bob,
Yuri, the scientific chiropractic
Ukrainian masseur,
and an old man who makes duck noises.

Snow covers East 4th Street
as I read, BORN IN TIBET,
by Rinpoche,
in which he suggests
'Who Am I?'
is not a question...

and I wonder what
the stones of Surmang
have in common
with those of Second Avenue...
This is not a question too.

I shall cook me bacon, Lord,
where no one can find me.

I shall cook myself an omelet
and think about my soul, "It's

all right to wait alone."
I've cooked myself an omelet

sitting in the snow
and my mind was a pigeon

grinding pebbles in its beak.
I've cooked myself an omelet

on your coals, Lord,
but I shall pound my glass

into the bar and watch my image
fold in upon itself

before I become a leprechaun
and reminisce...

*"Put a man alone on a stage
and you have infinite possibilities.
Two, and you've the limits of civilization."*

Then I stepped out of myself
dripping wet,
nothing consummated,
all smiles and similes

and the smallest man I'd ever seen
from Dallas
blessed me like the Pope!

Dear Milton,

14 hrs at the typewriter!
How do you do it?
I think about you in that white room
beside the giant rubber plant
framed by a wall-sized window
as light descends
        on Kips Bay
        like
        STORM OVER TOLEDO,
you,
      writing
like one of the elements
while I can't find anything to say
that takes more than a minute
to jot down!
            You,
at the machine
while I stalk around wondering
why writers become paranoid,
(because no one buys or applauds
their work?   no grants
no fellowships?
no honorary degrees?)
Dreiser
could never please his critics
or his friends.
And when did I become so wolfish?

Dear Ruth,

We're agreed on this much:
the fact of caring,
the shape of our thighs and lips
testing for congruence,
but in this proof
when your passion rises,
mine remains watchful,
or the reverse...
during which I move inside you
like a lapse of memory.

Shall we sleep?
Shall we speak our minds
and still be careful of words
that swell in our throats,
these ghosts
that escape through gaps
we make with our mouths,
in your long dress,
in my heavy coat?

A stone Buddha from Da Nang
sits on my TV
I bought him on the promenade
after eating sweet and sour
dog-meat in the shadow
of the New Guinea Trader
orange stacks
tied up at the quay
behind venereal short-time
shacks vibrating with Marines...

I balance him in the palm
of one hand
and prepare to read **THE LITERARY MIND
AND THE CARVING OF DRAGONS**

Nietzsche wrote from the madhouse in Jenna
he'd learned more from lust than literature
but the lasting sound
of untreatable clap
is all I got from Mimi

A good freeze with no rush.
Procaine cut.

What is America coming to!
What am I coming to!

Menken knew,
defined the species as

BOOBUS AMERICANUS

a bird that goose-steps
before it flies.

Will there be blemishes on my face
  in the morning,
will I have all my teeth,
  all my hair:
    will there be enough
love in Beauty for the Beast...
will she touch him?
    Words, Names, Places
    pinwheel,
refuse to fix themselves.
The face I see
smiles at me and vanishes.
It's done.
I'm too high to eat the meal
and here is the waitress
waiting at the table to be paid.

Turning onto Great Jones Street
full moon through magnesium light
petrifies the stones,
mortifies my shadow.

I am Dr. Frankenstein's son
returning to find his father's monster
rigid in a violet gas.
                An awkward beast
                who craves affection
                more than sex,
I ask,
        "Why should I bring him to life again?"

And the answer comes:
                "Because he is
                your brother,
                but his mother
                was lightning!"

We both wear diving gear...
she in a bikini.
I follow her around deck
but lose her in a companionway.
Did she swim off?
Did the hull-plates open
and she shoot out of my dream
like a torpedo?

Fragments of her after-image
on East 5th Street:
shop girls emerging
from 8 o'clock doorways
refreshed by dreamless sleep.

I want them.
I want them all
around me like tendrils,
to confuse their limbs with mine.

–What is desire?

–ENERGY THAT MOVES FROM A SOURCE OF HEAT
IN A PARTICLE TO A THERMAL TONE IN THE
COSMOS

–How does it work?

–THE ACCUMULATION OF AFFINITIES. THERE ARE
THINGS THAT CAN BE SEEN AND THINGS THAT CAN'T

–Does desire create a mode of seeing?

–YES. BUT NOT THROUGH DESPAIR

*–Where is the distortion in my relationships
that I keep returning to despair?*

–IN THE ADDED TUMULT, IN THE BANG-UP WORLD,
IT IS THERE

–What shall I do?

–BANG THE STARS INTO A CAN AND TAME THEIR
TIME INTO A CUP FOR YOUR TEARS

On the subway I read Kawabata
is dead,
a suicide at 72.
In a gray building on East 28th
men jam the stairs to apply
for jobs at
          WORLD WIDE
             DETECTIVE AGENCY,
while,
down the hall,
at METROPOLITAN ACADEMY
I ask my class:
*"Can an anorexic adolescent girl
still find romance at the movies?"*

A Lolita in black tights
announces
she's given up black magic
for psychology
          and questions
          my motives.
The class agrees
that I am suspect and votes
unanimously to discuss
instead:

MID-LIFE CRISIS FOR THE PEEPING TOM!

Why did I sign that contract to play piano
at the bar?

"A bit of jazz," he said. *"You know,*
something like, YOU GO TO MY HEAD?
It draws the college crowd."

What could I have been thinking
smiling as I did finger exercises in the air?
I can't play a note!

I phoned the female vocalist
whose manager informed me
she'd run off to the coast
and by six o'clock
had wound myself into a perfect frenzy
staring at the keyboard
trying to work out a few stand-up jokes.

FLUID MECHANICS
HEAT TRANSFER

THERMODYNAMICS...
    my fingers aching
    for a continuous
    thread:
        "Even radium
        gets tired of itself
        and changes into
        another element."

Why is it easier
to scramble
than unscramble
an egg,
      and everything
      I touch
become a battleground
for precedent?
I can feel whole armies on their bellies
crawling out of time, out of mind...

On a good day it's most satisfying to be free
not to search...
                especially for a fisherman
                in a net shirt
                on his way to the fishing ground
Should I be worried my shorts
don't fit
                (as if my fantasy
                might find me unstylish)?
And if I held her
in my thought
would it affect the movement
of the waves?

I am a rower who has swallowed his oarlocks!

A jellyfish
            between rocks
            strewn with gull shit
            and shells
gulls
have dropped:
                        I stop
            at the end of the spit
            to watch
fishermen
returning with
            their rakes and traps
            in a wake
            of broken cloud.
They wave
and involve me
            in the dream
            of their quiescence.
That night
at the movies
            I smell salt
            on the coat of the man
            in front of me...
he must
be a fisherman.
            On my way
            to work the next day
I'm amazed
by the smell of the sea on lower Broadway.

My days
a lattice
work O my
creepers
your
suppleness
on my work.
Wind
my clock
I hear you
ticking
my evasions
into no matter.
I will
build me a boat
of bullet-wood
lignum vitae
and sail down to
Monkey River.
I will drop my hook
in the mouth
of the sea.
I will open
my intimate
baggage
with magnets
and draw out
my desire
as mosquitoes
draw blood
off the coast
of Belize.

Dear Bob,

      Tomorrow I'll be 31 and feel
like Ari-of-the-Blessed-Memories
because all I want to know
is what Galileo,
              on his knees,
muttered under his breath
away from the waxy ears
of the court:
it might've been,
              "We are alone
              in a strange place."

      About my own view
let me confess
I imagine consciousness
as a grid
that changes
as it moves along a sliding scale
the face of which determines
our desires and beliefs
and has a certain resonance
when stretched
and held against the wind
like a perforated membrane…

Chuan-tzu called it,
"the mind of the lute,"

as if there were a wind
that passed through us

and we were each tuned
at different intervals.

                    Liu Hsieh says
                    a man can take his songs

                    and the force to shape them
                    from the air

                    once he hears the madness
                    of jade,

                    a lasting sound within
                    the silence of that stone.

As she spoke
I remembered being a child
in a space ship
frightened
among the stars
hiding my face
in the upholstery.

"For so long you've been leaving
even as you came,
on the verge of departing
even as you fell in love:
light years between
your touch and your feelings
and this is what comes of it,
these words
and what's left
of the voyage,
a slight warp
of the skeleton
from pressure and speed,
a small defraction
between your parts
which leaves them sometimes
aching."

Summer,
       the inquisitorial length
       of its frustration
       like Torquemada's nose,
       or Gogol's
       on his deathbed
       ablaze with leeches.

In a bookstore
       I watch her kneel,
       am stunned like an ambulance
       stuck in traffic...
              THE LINE OF HER LEG
       THROUGH DIAPHANOUS CLOTHES!

       (July had been
       a swampy vision
       but August finds me dumb
       my own olfactotum a bloodwurst
          after too much sun)
en route from her toes
she bends
       OH GOD!

       I go home
       thumb through **Zen Archery**,
       masturbate
       and wax invisible...

I've come back with messages from space,
Cynthia.

Mars is barren
but the souls of old reprobates
live in the Crab Nebula
where they generate light at regular intervals.

We have projected pictures of our nakedness
against the stars
and not one word back about our private parts.

Listening to birds this morning
I'm profoundly sad.
I can hear water in the mountains rushing
underneath the ground, wind in the trees.

It's not a bad feeling really
but it seems I've traveled so far to get here.

A little girl
in a red dress
falls down
in dandelions
laughing at
her own clumsiness…

at first
I think her an image
among images, then
see she's the whole poem.

THE CRY OF MERLIN

-for Carol

For what the stone expressed reminded me
of Merlin's life in the forest, after he had
vanished from the world. Men still hear his
cries, so the legend runs, but they cannot
understand or interpret them.

C.G. Jung, *MEMORIES, DREAMS, REFLECTIONS.*

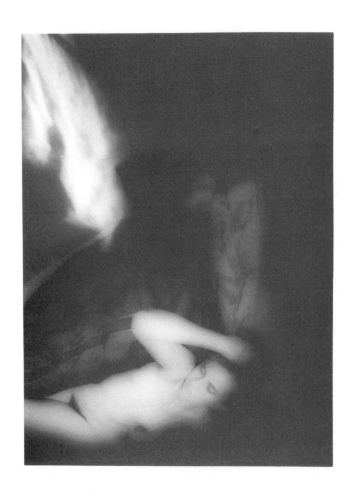

*

NERUDA'S voice
rises from the page
grieving for

LORCA, ALBERTI and MAYAKOVSKY

likens them
to a river, a mountain and a crystal,
and himself
        to a valley
with subterranean waters
pooling at its heart.
It is night.
I ride through the dark
on a bus
past little boxes
of light,
        in awe
    of this solitude
            I call
            my life.

*

Listen, Carol...

I want to say,
            "I love you!"

but it has a shell
around it
that breaks in my mouth

I pick the splinters
  from my throat
  and tongue

then say it...

the words have blood on them

*

My father's name was
Bernard.
He fucked up
in certain ways
but was a good man,
gave me what he could.
My mother's name was
Charlotte.
She fucked up, too,
but carried me
in her womb
and afterward
tried to keep in touch.
These were my parents,
Charlotte
and Bernard. They
fought but never
apologized,
died young and
left me behind like
a clue
at the scene
of a crime. Bernard
and Charlotte
a long time dead
and buried
inside me. I am
their tomb.
Charlotte and
Bernard. My mother
and father who
laugh when I insist
I'm nobody's baby now.

PUER AETERNUS

I thought I could hide
between your skirts, your legs,
your lips,
in your house, over breakfast
sipping coffee...
but there's a force
inside that will not
let me rest,
a whirlwind
from which a voice
cries out:
"Did you expect
suffering to cease
because you have all this,
as if these blessings
were personal?"

How can I say it
without scaring you?
The god
who speaks through me
is merciless,
a heart
too big for
my chest.

BLACK HOLE
BOOGIE

I get hungry when I'm broke
stuff myself with muffins
and scribble notes
to remind me
that there are worse fates
than getting too fat
for your clothes...

I sit in coffee shops
over buttered rolls
watching my dignity
at the Hammond
in a red shirt
and bow tie
circle
            a Black Hole
            singing

    "On The Road Again"

            to the sustained
            ovation
            of exploding
            stars

ALONE
WITH THE CORPSE MOTHER

She smiles but can't raise her head.
I sit at the edge of her linen bier
and tell her I miss her.
Decaying but not quite dead,
red lips alive
with irony,
      she says:
              DEATH IS NOT THE ISSUE
              EVEN DEATH IS ALIVE.
The corpse cannot exist alone but
drawing strength from my reluctance
to let her go,
      takes my hand
      then stares
      at her image
      in my eyes
fixed on a hole in her chest
through which worlds emerge
and disappear.
I whisper:
      "Let the body
      of this illusion perish..."
drop her hand and feel her dissolve
into a darkness
from which she will again rise
as the midnight sun
      of Isis,
unseen light of Self and Soul.

*

A Dutch lithograph shows
the old Alchemist's study;
a disarray of folios
and clothes,
curtains in that sealed space
ballooned
as if they held
the wind...

the windless room
of a private man
for whom
women
have always been
containers of the mystery
whose solution
he is—
        a bachelor
        wed to
        the solitary uses of his sperm

PRAYER
++
BEFORE
DROWNING

At last I understand
how we shed

our lives in time,
peel off outrage

terror
and despair

like wet clothes
after a freezing rain.

Nothing to fear.

We shall all sink
 back into

the unconscious
of this world

your warm
matrix,

Isis,
patroness of seamen!

*

Dark women are in the sea
our own depth in the depth of the world.

They
are the swimmers who take us down.

Trees
in the rain
are drenched in this sea
as are grass,
        stones,
        cars on the highway.

Dark women swim through them
and into this room
saying,
        *"Desire is the measure
        of all things."*

I tell them I want to know
what is already here but hidden
and ask them to connect you
that way to me.

*

Orpheus
loses Eurydice
to return
      with the vision
      of Eurydice
which dissolves like a word
on his tongue

So he goes down again to
the forge
      where forms
      are made
to emerge
with a song that contains
a moth
playing at the source
of desire—
      a river of fire
that flows both ways

THE CRY OF MERLIN

The voice is not the word
though it shapes
and contains it
rising from a fire
that makes shadows dance
on the wall of our cranium.
There is another voice
beneath sound (such as
we hear in dreams
with an inner ear)
that grows so loud it
can move through us
with a force that makes
us speak in tongues.
At times we are aware
of a question
coiled in the silence
where breath begins
which can be answered
only with an inner voice
that will not speak
until we are dumbfounded.
To be found dumb is to
perish into what we hear.

CAFE DE
LA PARROQUIA

Morning light
arches in the colonnade.

Looking down his nose
the waiter pours
       cafe con leche
from two steaming kettles
while patrons
wanting refills
       tap their spoons.

I recall
my first visit
       to Vera Cruz,
a boy
intoxicated with his life,
tap my glass
and watch
       my skeleton
dance
down Avenida Independencia.

MEMORY IS
ADJECTIVE
TO TIME

I have walked a Mayan city
in the jungle
        near Benque Viejo—

a syntax
of chambers
walls and patios
under half an inch of earth

buried
        in my mind
        like a message
        waiting

                to be smuggled back
                into the world

APOSTLE OF THE FLOATING WORLD

Flatbush
Insurgentes
Le Loi
saloons
push carts
women in doorways

on every street I walk
someone calls

"Oye, Pablo,
que bien estoy!"

and I am young again
wondering
how
to create a corridor

of words

through which
to approach
what remains unexplored

PONT L'ARCHIVECHE

This evening I'm surprised
anew
by the way light
alludes to

    an exile

    wherein
    a world of which
    I cannot speak
    is glorified

END OF THE CENTURY

Birds
outside our bedroom window
wake me from a dream.
                    Sun still low,
my wife dresses, brings me coffee, wants to know
if I'd care to walk toward
                    Sevres-Babylon?

                    *

On our way
we pass old Messiaen on Rue Seguier
carrying a portfolio.
                    He pauses
under the outline
of a harpist from an Egyptian tomb
stenciled over a doorway
listening
            to that dream of Empire
            still in the womb at Invalides,
            pricking
            the sky
at the center of Concorde—
ears tuned
for footsteps
                    on streets
                    Hitler walked
                    alone
                    addressing statues.

                    *

Rumors of spring in Place Maubert.
The air is alive
with doves
falling
through
the Tuilleries

like a poem   by Apolinaire,
who saw Jesus as an aviator.
Crowds mill around San Sulpice.
Gurdjieff,
who ate with his eyes,
is a breadcrumb at La Coupole;
St. Exupery,
who perished in a plane,
flies over
the Pont de l'Archiveche,
a seagull,
on it's way to Ile St. Louis.

*

We spend the afternoon at the Marmottan
with its Monets and bare breasted sphinxes
shaped like my wife,
who turns
to kiss me.
Later, in the Maraise,
I cling to
the memory
of her body
like twilight on the shutters
of Rue Mahler.

TEMPLE OF THE BUDDHA'S FOOTPRINT

They surround him
with carved ivory
apply gold-leaf
to the image of one
whose palms
were inlaid with rebirth
whose toes
were all the same length
whose earlobes
sagged with long life
but only those
who have felt the knife
of his inward gaze
his fire
that burns up suffering
but
throws neither light
nor heat
know him
as peace calling out
to peace...
the smile of an empty bowl

REMEMBERING
SITA

At night I understand
your nails as frozen ponds
whose depth cannot be measured
and it makes me cry.

So I stand and repeat,
    "Standing...standing,"
walk and repeat,
    "Walking...walking,"
until I am purified
by 16 kinds of knowledge
like cool fingers on my brow.

Then I think again of your nails
the tender purple ring
around their white half-moons
and know I will always be sad.

*

* RAMA'S DREAM *

*

I reach for you beneath the sheets.
The skin of time asleep
touches my limbs
and for an instant I believe it's you,
as you were,
touching me
as I had been.

I will always love you in this peculiar way.

DRAGON SMOKE

The dragon smoke means that a leap has taken place...that leap can be described as a leap from the conscious to the latent intelligence and back again...

Robert Bly, *AMERICAN POETRY*

A WORD ABOUT THE SLEEP-MAN

I read my daughter stories
the Otoe
told their children
to prepare them for the Sleep Man
explaining how
        coyote became a thief
        little white rabbit got pink eyes
details she will need
to find her way through the landscape
of her life

I am like every father who
tries to explain
the seven stars
in the Big Dipper,
are also
        seven clans
        (to which she is related)
        seven angels
        seven spirits
        who will advise her in distress
        comfort her in mourning
        join her in celebration

        seven eyes
        that look back in time
        to the place of first things
        where horse and buffalo
        racing to determine who was fastest
        left a trail of dust that became
        the Milky Way

        seven kisses
        that wait for her in heaven
        where all events are marked
        before they are recorded

        "Yah-wah   shee-geh!"

THE MAN IN THE MOON

The story goes that Running Antelope
became the Man in the Moon
trying to rescue his wife Little Hill
abducted by a wicked Chief
whose power proved so great
that the Water Spirit
had to help the brave escape
into the night sky

I ask myself
if Running Antelope
still searches for his wife
wonder if she misses him
does she recognize his face
gazing down
and take comfort

looking at my daughter
and my wife asleep
I know the answer
recognize my own face
as the one
reflected
in water

SACRED WORLD

The flowers of the Spring Moons vanish more quickly
than those of the Summer.
                              Both
die into the rainbow
                    Too-loo-lah
where their colors
come alive again after the rain.

I learn as I go
how to read the book of the world.

How many flowers does it take
Tululah?

UNDERSTANDING THE LONG-BODY

Running through Cole's Wood
red sugar maples

their molten core covering
my path like volcanic ash

I think about fathers and sons
how they break each others hearts

the child who wrestled me down
in last night's dream

alive in the long-body
of my stride at fifty-five

past pines that watched
Iroquois track white men

I think about that fresco in Pompeii
in which a child at a mirror

sees himself as an old man
the long-body of father and son

cutting both ways a lesson Rome
 learned too late

"My father and I are one"
dogs me through a cedar grove

where woodpeckers hammer
the last golden light to dead limbs

CHRISTMAS IN GLENS FALLS

at the Unitarian Universalist Church
a man in a Rudolph hat
complete with electric nose,
welcomes us

the Children's Choir
is followed by an elder whistling
 "What Child Is This?"

to remind us
of the child reborn in
each of us

while
uptown
among the Methodists
a transsexual tenor
in full drag
announces she
will no longer answer
to the name
of Robert

MEDICAL MIRACLES

1

Over a bagel and coffee
at Cool Beans

my brother informs me
his heart is leaking

and the echo-cardiogram
indicates

that one of these days
he'll have to install

a pig valve
or a prosthesis which works

like a Ping-Pong ball
in a basket

"Surely we can
do better than that," he says

considering the huge advances
in medicine

billions in research spent by Sandoz
and Dupont

surely if he can just live
long enough

he might one day take a pill
and turn into a six foot

blue-eyed Aryan
named Hans

2

"See that guy
        by Shop n'Save
Yeah
        that one
    the Viking in Lederhosen
would you believe
    he used to be
        a short
            overweight
paranoid-delusional-schizophrenic
    with a mitral
        prolapse
    and the woman
        next to him
    the one who looks
        like Madonna
            she used to be
                his wife."

AFTER LINES BY ROQUE DALTON

What do you do when you realize
your enemy is smarter than you

has a better grip on the world
which reflects his longing

answers his desires
while it turns back your own?

Either you die or let go
of your enemy and the world—

your conception of them
as friends

who will come to love you
in time.

Time is running out
and maybe the world was made

by your enemy in his image
not yours.

Maybe he is godlike
(a possibility which you can't

abide or forgive)
and that divine spark

you thought belonged to you
always resided in him. While

you sat at home wondering
what to do—he did.

What choice is there but
to die or let go

of what you considered
your birthright—

the spellbinding displays
of your own mind

that time has proven
to be steeped in darkness.

Maybe you must die into
your assumptions

in order to embrace what
embraces you—

a world perched
on a column of turtles

unseen but suspected
by everyone.

EARTH, WIND, & FIRE

on a Saturday afternoon
a man in his 55th year
stands outside a record store
under a yew tree considering
          the difference between
          decline and
deconstruction

                    Credence Clearwater
blasts
through speakers above
the sign
          SOUNDS OF SOUTH STREET
kids browse racks inside sit on boxes
planted with coleus and impatiens
on either side of
an open door
                    they don't see him
                    open his chest to touch his heart
                    then point with bloody fingers
                    at a cloud that blocks
                    the sun
                              seem concerned
                              about the vaginas
                              falling from
                              the sky
                                        or hear him shout
                                        above
                              Hootie & the Blow Fish

          "Everything is afterbirth!"

EL SUEÑO DE RAZON

Reason sleeps in the virtual
caves of
        cyberspace

where
the sun is rolled
like dung
up a mountainside by
a man
        beheaded
        and restored
again and
again
without
consequence

SUMMER IN THE GATINEAU

land of once fierce Outawaise
                  and Hurons
haunted by blackrobed Jesuits
who believed they could
come to no better end
than martyrdom
at the hands
of the heathen
who were
finally convinced
to abandon their barricades
 for a heaven
where they could neither smoke
hunt nor make love

I watch the lake
and identify its wild inhabitants
                  a pair of hummingbirds
                    sucking at orange gladiolas
                  a fierce red squirrel
                    who uses the deck as a bridge
                  the song sparrow vibrating
                    on the tip of the same spruce
                    every morning

the anonymous hand
that wrote
                  FUCK THE WORLD
                        on the Ecole wall
                        of St. Pierre de Wakefield

LAC ST. PIERRE

in the pine-studded lap
of the Gatineau Hills
water
feathered by wind
a sparrow's tail
on the limb of a blue spruce
trembling at the end
of its song
night falls on our cottage
by the lake
I dream of walking
past my father's house
which I can no longer enter
melt into my wife's
silk pajamas
then wake
to the loon
echoing through the woods
I don't have to see its dark wings
at the water's edge
long body breaking the surface
to remember
its heavy bones keep it low
take it down deeper
when it dives

THE HAIDA

on the other hand
believe the universe is

a box of souls
contained by
ever
diminishing
boxes

as if
the infinite
were measurable
with finite
tools: *how many angels*
              can dance on the head
              of a pin
is not
a question but a locus
of awareness

a point
in space
from which time flows

"...what a marvel
is this point!"
said Leonardo
who observed that everything we see
is contained by light rays
converging
on a dot

in back
of the eye

Leonardo
tried to grasp the Idea
behind the physical event
    (How many angels
    can dance
    on the head of
    a pin
        is not a question
        but a mystery in which
        the greater is contained
        by the lesser)
haunted by flight
he praised the nest in which Icarus
was born
        conceived of
a bird-like creature driven by the soul
of a man
        and alluded in his notebook
        to the airplane
While his fellow painters were drunk
on perspective Leonardo
studied the proportions
of the swallow
        thought about
a childhood dream
in which the tail of a kite
brushed his
lips
    looked up at night
    to find
        the starry sky
        had entered him

LECTIO DIVINA

Clement Greenberg found Miro

*"...composed of two elements, one ludicrous,
the other fearful."*

               a vision
               emerging from Renaissance
               grottoes
(a miasma,
      grotto-esque)
               into the work of Valesquez
               and Goya,
                       that haunts Picasso
                       even in his rage of bulls
                       and centaurs

something subversive
in certain painters
through the early decades of
our century

that will mushroom
later
as
    Hiroshima

we see Canadian painters of the 30's and 40's
whose work on canvas
is lifeless
        snow-capped
        trees on empty streets
        backlit or shaded
        in ochres
what the culture held onto
until its young ones
returned from Europe
with images
too difficult to bear
that of a dying German paratrooper
an improbable flying object
downed as much by
arrogance
as war
        bodies
        curled around each other
        outside Bergen-Belsen
        like commas
        in a wordless
        sentence

DRAGON SMOKE

mist drifts down the lake
　　thickens into a cloud
　　sun can't penetrate
floating houses on the other side
remind me of Thailand
running the Mekong
　to the Golden Triangle
　families in junks
　Buddha caves where pilgrims
　come
　　　　close to Cambodian
　　　　refugee camps
poppy fields
overflowing
with Meo
　　　　itinerant
　　　　　opium
　　　　　　growers
　　　　　　　from Laos...
　　　　　　　　　　the veil shifts
　　　　　　　　　　　　iridescent threads
　　　　　　of moisture
　　　　　　　hang from trees
"It's like another world," she says,
I agree
　　　　watch a gold finch
　　　　disappear
into what by noon
becomes
　　　　a drop
　　　　　　　at the end
　　　　　　　of a leaf

CAVERNES LA FLECHE

Earliest accounts of creation
declare that our ancestors lived

in a state of perfect knowledge
could stare into the heart of heaven

until fearful gods blinded them
to all but the buried memory

of their origin
in search of which they crawled

down dark passages
toward images of bison

deer and woolly mammoth
galloping by torch light

flank and fetlock
fitted to the jutting surface

of a rock-hewn womb
from which blind

and forgetful men might be
born a second time

into what
lives unseen inside them

GROUNDLESSNESS

1)

Miro
clings to images
as if they are real
until 1922
when he paints
                    THE FARM
which Hemingway buys
to remind him of
                    the Catalan
                    landscape
but fails to see
      in the house without walls
            a tree rooted in a dark hole
                  the vision of
                  groundlessness
      at the center of
this painting

Once Miro glimpses it
he gives up the frame
and often
                  the horizon
lets
      biomorphs
            float
                  swallows of love
                  their song
                  UPSIDE DOWN
                  in his heart

2)

Miro never wholly
gives up the image
or relinquishes
gravity
            like Rothko
            and Gorky
or Guston who
lets his compositions
                        float
untethered
even by the darkness
within
            their blacks
            and bloody ochres
held
by a light
that renders them
weightless
            like Rothko
            a suicide
            in grays and blacks
            Gorky hanging from a beam
            in his garage...

while Miro
continues to walk a tightrope
of staffless notes
blossoming like wildflowers
in his colorfield

3)

For Guston
composition is a continual argument
between
reason and wonder
that art
could contain his terror
yet leave
nothing solid
to stand on...

           he spends hours
           discussing Dostoevsky
           with John Cage
                     at the Automat
                     with Morton Feldman
                     enflamed
                     by parallels between
                     painting and
                     music

          content becomes
          transparent to
          process
               a creature trapped
               in his own
               creation
                     beyond consolation
                     he abandons abstraction
                     to paint images of old shoes

"this train makes no stops..."
                                    Miro

At eighty Malcolm Cowley wrote about
Renoir painting magnificently

the brush strapped to his arm
"for years after he was crippled by arthritis"

Goya deaf and half-blind produced new work
through several layers of spectacles

When Matisse could no longer hold a brush
he cut forms out of colored paper

Da Vinci ended his life at Close-Lucé
designing weapons for Francois I

then wept on his deathbed
that he had not worked harder at his art

"The great ones develop as they get older"
said Miro who worked until his death at ninety

But what of Henry Miller who in his eighties
struggled to *"Not do"*

Stevens for whom the colors
"deepened and grew small."

Eliot who looked back to see his years
like *"stones that cannot be deciphered"*

Pound whose last written words
beg us to *"forgive what I have made"*

THE RIG VEDA

conceives of creation from
the unconditioned ground
    of *mind-before-thought*

I too had this idea
in 1953
at the age of twelve on the corner
of Flatbush Avenue and Empire
Boulevard
        at the gated entrance
        to Ebbets Field
        a week after The Giants
        won the pennant

and knew it wasn't mine

BROOKLYN

Inside my house patriarchs
are sleeping

beards hanging in the hallway
beside their commandments

I am in the eaves watching
gypsies across the street

someone strops a razor
on my tie

the paisley bleeds
and there are sirens in the night

(one for every nail
in the bedpost of the dreamer)

a sheep is ready now
for shearing under an arc light

the space turns red above
its bleating but I never see

the animal naked
standing still or moving

DOMESTICITY

Zoro by the door chews his bone
Ben Webster on NPR
plays *Making Whoopie*
my wife in the bedroom talks
on the phone

I recall other lives
on the lower East Side
in Cholon
nights in smoky clubs
listening to Eddie Jefferson
wandering Belizean bush
over empires buried
under half an inch
of earth...
                    until my daughter
                    wonders what I'm doing
                    alone in the dark
                    asks, *Daddy, are you all right?*

                    Sure, I say
                              knowing she's afraid
                              I've gone too far away
                              and might never
                              come back

WHAT IS THE FACE OF TIME IN REPOSE

like Vishnu
            asleep on
            a coiled serpent
            floating in a milky sea

I forget what I know
all that I have done or read
            vanishes

each night
in the pit of forgetfulness

I raise a monument
            to Buddha
            and Osiris

a stupa of
dreams
            (inside of which
            everything
            lost is
            found)

                        and dance
                        on its burning tip

"someone in some future time will think of us"

looking at the night sky
Sappho said
the stars
cover their faces
when the full moon
turns earth silver
first poet astronaut
to reverse perspective
unlike Persephone who
discovered resurrection
by sinking into Hades
Sappho praised memory
over immortality
looking down from above
at a small globe
surrounded
by lacy clouds
so like a child's
plaything

"One must participate with joy in the sorrows
of this world."
                    Joseph Campbell

on the porch at night
listening to the high insect thrum
that comes at the end
of summer

                    he remembered
                    being a child
afraid of the dark
calling parents who seldom came
to his bedside

                    now he tip-toes
through the house
past the dog asleep in his crate
his daughter curled up with the cat

slips in beside his wife who grasps
his hand without waking

PAUL PINES grew up in Brooklyn around the corner from Ebbet's Field and passed the early 60's on the Lower East Side of New York. He shipped out as a Merchant Seaman—spending '65-'66 in Vietnam. In 1970, he opened a jazz club, The Tin Palace—located on the corner of 2nd Street and Bowery—which became a cultural watering hole for the better part of the '70s. It provided the setting for his first novel, *The Tin Angel* (Wm Morrow, 1983). During this period, Pines traveled in Central America where he became aware of the genocidal policy targeting Guatemalan Mayans—the basis for his second novel, *Redemption* (Editions du Rocher, 1997). His poems have appeared in *New Directions #37, First Intensity, Cafe Review, Pequod, Ironwood, IKON, Prairie Schooner, Mulch* and *Contact II.* He now resides in Glens Falls, New York, with his wife, Carol, and daughter, Charlotte where he teaches at Adirondack Community College and coordinates the Lake Geroge Jazz Weekend.

JOSEPHINE SACABO is an internationally acclaimed photographer who now lives and works in New Orleans. A monograph of her work was published in Paris by Editions Marval and her next book, an illustrated *Pedro Paramo,* published by the University of Texas Press was published in October, 2002.